Tikki Tikki Tembo

By Carol Kaplan-Lyss
Curriculum Ideas by Helen R. Marner

Table of Contents

Cover Photo: Steve Gross
Cover Design: Jeff Richards
Illustrations: Kathy Mitter
CD: Carol Kaplan-Lyss, Judy Medoff, and Michael Lyss

Printed in the United States of America

978-1-5586-3108-3

MILLIKEN
P.O. Box 802 • Dayton, OH 45401
www.LorenzEducationalPress.com

NOTES TO THE TEACHER/DIRECTOR

This package is designed for use with young children. The musical is easy to prepare and perform. Even non-musical teachers will find it simple to prepare all aspects of the performance—from initially presenting the story to the children to the final production. Tracks 1-12 of the CD contain the music and lyrics. This CD can be placed in the listening center or the book corner for children to listen to as they read or play quietly. This is an easy way to teach children the songs. Tracks 13-30 contain the accompaniment only. These tracks can be used during an actual performance if musicians are not available.

The *Tikki Tikki Tembo* resource guide contains suggestions for preparation and performance. Note that it contains *suggestions* not *directions.* Feel free to modify the experience to fit the needs of your group. Add or delete characters as needed. Choose a strong reader to be the narrator, or read the narration yourself while the children act out the parts and sing the songs. You may assign songs to certain characters or your entire group can sing all the songs. If your group is very young, you may wish to simplify the musical by eliminating some songs. If you do so, add a little to the narration to replace lyrics that are important to the story line. These and other changes can make the experience more enjoyable for your group.

This musical is based on an ancient oriental folktale called *Tikki Tikki Tembo.* The suggested activities allow you to involve children in a multisensory learning experience. You may turn the experience into a cross-curricular unit on China as you help children explore art, music, literature, movement, science, and social studies in relationship to the characters, story, and culture of *Tikki Tikki Tembo.*

Tikki Tikki Tembo

LANGUAGE AND READING

Begin work on this musical play by reading the story of *Tikki Tikki Tembo* to the children. Talk about the concept of a folktale and discuss the fact that folktales can have different versions. Read the narration of this musical as an example of another version of the story. Perhaps the children can think of another way to tell the story and can experience the fun of storytelling for themselves. Some children will be able to write down their own version of the story and then illustrate it. Other children may simply write scribbles or a few letters they know with illustrations. The children can then "read" their stories to you or to the class. If you work with younger children, you might want to write down their version of the story and then have them illustrate it.

As another storytelling experience, begin a story and have the children take turns adding to it. If children have never had this "round-robin" kind of experience, they may be stilted until they feel comfortable and can let their imagination lead them.

The last line of the musical, "All's well that ends well," is called an *adage.* Explain that an adage is an expression many people understand because it has been repeated over the years. Suggest some adages the children might have heard and see if they know what they mean. (Some examples include *a bird in the hand is worth two in the bush, better late than never, the early bird catches the worm, now you're cooking with gas, that's the way the cookie crumbles,* and *two heads are better than one.*)

In the narration for this musical Tikki Tikki Tembo-No So Rembo-Icka Na Noo Na-Konna Ron Tombo's name is described as "long and honorable." Discuss the meaning of the word *honorable* with the children. Ask them to think of other things that might be considered honorable.

The Chinese language is very different from English. In Chinese, inflection determines what a word means. For example, the sound *ma* said in a high, even tone means mother. If the same sound is begun high and then lowered, it means to scold. If it starts low and ends high, it means hemp, a kind of twine. If the sound starts normally, dips low in the middle and rises in the end, it means horse. If possible, have someone who can speak Chinese visit your class. Ask him or her to share information about the oral and written language. If no one is available, you may want to find a recording of the Chinese language. (Play songs with Chinese lyrics if necessary.) After the children have listened to the language, show them the Chinese characters below. Tell the children that the Chinese use characters instead of an alphabet. Note that each character is somewhat like a picture. Discuss the fact that a Chinese person has to know 5,000 characters just to read a newspaper. Have the children try to copy some of the simpler symbols. The children might have fun coming up with their own pictures to represent words they know.

| people | up | down | mountain | small | big |

Tikki Tikki Tembo

MOVEMENT AND DRAMATIC PLAY

Young children enjoy exploring experiences with their bodies as well as their minds. Before the children act out *Tikki Tikki Tembo*, encourage them to discuss actions portrayed in the story, act them out, and try to feel the characters' emotions. Talk about feelings and how we use our faces and bodies to show emotions. Ask children to think about what it would be like to fall into a deep well with water in it. Have them pretend to balance on the edge of a well and then tumble in. Next they can pretend to be washing clothes by a stream or flying a kite on a windy day. Have them act out other situations they remember from the story.

In the musical, the old man hobbles to the well.

Make a list of other words that show movement, such as *walking, running, tumbling, loping, rolling, reeling,* and *hobbling.* Have the children act out the words on the list.

In China the people practice a form of physical exercise and mental control called *t'ai chi ch'uan.* This gentler form of the martial arts is usually done outdoors in the morning or during lunch breaks and is done in groups. Lead the children through some slow controlled exercises that include flexing and relaxing muscles and balancing. You may want to begin the school day with a short period of this type of exercise.

SOCIAL STUDIES

The tale of *Tikki Tikki Tembo* serves as a wonderful introduction to a unit on China. As they read or hear the story, the children will note some facts about Chinese culture. It is important to talk about modern China versus China in the past. Show some pictures of modern China and the Chinese people. If there are any Chinese people in the school or community, they may be willing to offer a rich look into their native land and its traditions and customs. UNICEF shops, found in many cities, offer culture kits on China for classroom use. These kits can include clothes and examples of ceremonial objects for hands-on learning.

Festivals were an important part of life in old China. The lunar New Year celebration was one of the major festivals in old China. On the Chinese New Year, everyone had a birthday and became a year older. Therefore a baby that was born a month before the New Year would become one year old after one month of life. Choose a child whose birthday is late in the year and determine whether that child would have been considered to be a different age in old China.

The Chinese New Year is considered to be a time to clean house and put on new clothes. Have a room

cleaning session in your classroom or in your house center.

During the New Year celebration, Chinese children are usually given money in special red envelopes. Red is considered to be a lucky color by the Chinese. Have a "lucky day" in your room. Give each child a "lucky" penny. Have the children make rubbings of their pennies. Then have each child wrap the penny up in red tissue paper and hang it with red yarn on the "lucky money tree." (This can be a tree branch standing in a coffee can full of sand.) At the end of your study of China and following the performance of the musical, the children can take their lucky pennies home.

There are many other activities you can do on Lucky Day. You may want to serve fortune cookies for snack or in the house center. The children may also enjoy learning the Chinese Fortune Game. To create this game for your class, you will need a juice can, ten craft sticks, a marker, and a sheet of paper. On each stick write one numeral from one to ten. Then have the class help you write down on paper one fortune to correspond to each number. To play the game, each child shakes the can up and down gently. The number on the first stick to fall out of the

Tikki Tikki Tembo

can will correspond to the number of that person's fortune. Read that fortune from the sheet of paper.

Another way to celebrate the Chinese New Year is to prepare a special Chinese meal for the children to eat. There are many different Chinese foods to choose. You may want to make the fried rice recipe listed in the SCIENCE section of this resource book. Have the children try to eat the meal with chopsticks that can be purchased in bulk at import shops and some grocery stores. You may want to serve tea with the meal. If you are not able to cook in your room, serve pieces of rice cakes that can be purchased in the grocery store. These are somewhat dry and might need some kind of jelly spread on them.

One of the highlights of the Lunar New Year festival is a large dragon that travels through the streets. Your class can create its own giant dragon. The children can make the head out of a box decorated with many colors of crepe paper. One child can wear this head and all the other children can get underneath a red blanket or piece of cloth to form the dragon's body. (Illus. 1) Have a parade down the hall or on the playground.

The Festival of Lanterns is also part of the New Year celebration. Each child can make a lantern out of construction paper by cutting slits in the paper, folding it around, and gluing it. The child can then attach crepe paper strips to the lantern. (Illus. 2) Hang these lanterns from strands of Christmas tree lights to make the room very festive.

The BIBLIOGRAPHY lists some books that will be helpful when planning any kind of Chinese New Year celebration.

The next few curriculum areas include ideas for continuing the study of Chinese culture in those specific areas. As you read through these ideas, you can decide which of them you want to develop with your class.

Illus. 1

Illus. 2

5   Tikki Tikki Tembo

MUSIC

Discuss the fact that a musical is different from a play because a musical is a story set to music. When the children have written or told their own stories, as suggested in the LANGUAGE section, they can make up a song to tell part of their story. This activity can also be done as a group.

Discuss the importance of a chorus. Talk about the fact that a chorus tells the audience many important facts that they need to know in order to understand a musical. During the performance of *Tikki Tikki Tembo*, most of the children in your class will be members of the chorus. Be sure that these children are made to feel as important as the actors.

You can form a Chinese orchestra to provide accompaniment during the musical. The orchestra members would be part of the chorus but would also play simple rhythm instruments. You can use regular classroom instruments, or the children can make special instruments for the occasion. Children can make simple tambourines from plastic margarine lids with jingle bells attached around the edge. (Illus. 3) Shakers are easy to create from toilet paper tubes. Put dried beans inside the tubes then cover the ends with paper. (Illus. 4) Sticks and pan lids can be hit together, and sandpaper-covered blocks can be rasps. You and the children will probably think of many other instruments to make. Be creative!

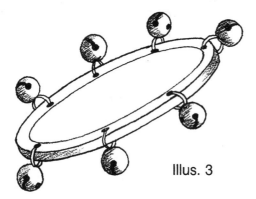

Illus. 3

Illus. 4

ART

The art center can become a very important area for experimenting with some traditional Chinese art forms. Children can try brush painting with black paint on white paper. They can also try the ancient art of making papercuts—creating a picture by cutting it out of one piece of paper that remains in one piece. (Illus. 5) The BIBLIOGRAPHY at the end of this guide lists books that are excellent sources for details on the art of papercuts.

There are many Chinese people who are experts at making sculptures. Children in China make little toys out of a salt dough. Some of the common forms made are snakes, pandas, tigers, and birds. To make salt dough, mix 1 cup salt with 2 cups flour and 1 cup water. (This makes enough dough for 8–10 children.) Knead this mixture. Give each child a small

Illus. 5

 Tikki Tikki Tembo

amount of dough to shape. After each child has created a shape, bake the shapes in a 325°F oven for about 30 minutes. (Note that smaller pieces cook faster.) After the shapes are cooked, the children can decorate them with colored markers.

During the musical the character Ping Ping flies a kite. The children may enjoy creating their own kites from brightly colored paper. The BIBLIOGRAPHY lists books that are helpful for this project.

Create an art center where the set and costumes for the musical can be created. If you choose to follow the costume suggestions in this book, the old shirts or pillowcases the children will wear can be painted and decorated in the art center. The old man's hat, his beard, the flowers, and the kite can be created in the center as well. The children can work together to build and paint the well, the tree, and the backdrop for the production.

You may choose to work with your group to design a program booklet for the audience. The program will vary according to the ability level of your group. The children can draw covers for these programs. If you plan a performance for the children's families, you may want to have each child draw a picture of himself or herself and write a little about the part he or she has in the performance. These programs make fun keepsakes for the children and their families. The words to the songs can also be included in the program. The children may wish to add other illustrations they feel are appropriate.

SCIENCE

Since this story deals with a well, talk about where water comes from and how we use it. (Where does the water that we drink and use in our homes come from? Does our area get water from a river, a well, or a reservoir? How does the water get from this place to our homes? How does that differ from the water source in this tale?) Be sure to discuss the fact that this is an old story and that most of the people of China today have other ways of getting water.

This musical can lead to a discussion on safety. In the musical the mother sends each of her sons to get the old man with the rope to free the child in the well. After Tikki Tikki Tembo-No So Rembo-Icka Na Noo Na-Konna Ron Tombo comes out of the well, the old man pushes water out of the boy. Discuss artificial respiration and how we use it to help someone who has been under water for a time. Compare it to the description of the old man trying to help Tikki Tikki Tembo-No So Rembo-Icka Na Noo Na-Konna Ron Tombo. Ask a member of the fire department or an emergency medical service to come and demonstrate how to employ artificial respiration and to discuss other important safety tips. Be sure to discuss precautions that should be taken when a child is near water.

As suggested in the SOCIAL STUDIES section, do some Chinese cooking with the class if possible. Talk about the foods the children in your group eat that are the same and different from the usual Chinese diet. Discuss the fact that some foods are prepared differently in China. The Chinese use chopsticks to eat their food so they need food prepared in small pieces. Of course, the Chinese people rely on rice as their basic food. In this country, we eat many wheat and corn products. Have your group taste rice cakes and make a hot rice dish such as fried rice. You may also want to allow them to taste tea.

Chinese Fried Rice
(As adapted by Helen Marner)

3 T. oil
2 eggs (beaten)
3 cups prepared rice
1 t. salt
finely chopped broccoli (fresh or frozen)
Cooked, cut up chicken (optional)

Heat 1 tablespoon oil in electric wok or frying pan. Pour in eggs and as they set, transfer them to bowl. Break up eggs with fork. Add remaining oil and heat. Add rice and stir fry 2 to 3 minutes. Add salt, vegetables, and chicken. Stir fry 20 seconds. Add eggs. Cook until heated through. Serve in small styrofoam drinking cups. Fill about half full. Serves about 20 children as a snack.

REHEARSALS AND PERFORMANCE

Remember that preparing and performing this musical should be fun for everyone. The wonderful thing about presenting a musical with young children is that it doesn't have to be perfect. The unexpected usually adds flavor and interest. The process is definitely more important than the finished product.

It is important that the children feel comfortable in the room in which they will be performing. Allow them time to explore and practice in the area. Bring the children to the area where the audience will sit. Move to the performance area and talk in a normal tone of voice. Discuss the fact that in order for the audience to hear the performance, the children need to use strong voices when they sing. It will be especially important for the narrator, if it is a child, to practice using a louder voice. Stress the fact that the children must listen carefully since they will be picking up cues from the narrator. The narrator's words will help them to know what comes next and when they are to sing or move on the stage.

Try not to over-rehearse. Instead of practicing the entire play over and over, allow students to practice small parts separately so that other children don't lose interest or become bored while waiting for their parts. You will probably only need to go through the entire musical three times. The last of those three run-throughs can be the dress rehearsal.

On the day of the dress rehearsal, try to have a small audience so the children can get used to performing in front of people. This will also give you an idea of whether there are any children who still feel uncomfortable performing and need some special help. Never force a child to perform. If rehearsals are low key and fun, most children will want to participate. If there is a child who can't peform for some reason, you can make that child a stage manager who helps behind the scenes.

The dress rehearsal includes everything you are planning to do during the actual performance. If you are planning to give a little speech first, then do it during this rehearsal. Include the person who is going to play the music or use the CD as accompaniment. Rehearse the bow-taking that will take place when the musical is over.

On the day of the performance when the children are in costume and ready to perform, take a few minutes to talk to them about some of the feelings they may be having, such as anxiety and excitement. Assure them that you will be with them and will give them cues if they should forget something. Discuss how proud they should be of what they have learned and accomplished.

If possible have someone videotape the performance. The children will enjoy seeing themselves, and the viewing of the videotape can become a cast party. It will serve as an opportunity to talk about and reinforce the experience.

COSTUME IDEAS

Mother: 2 pillowcases, a long thin piece of fabric or a scarf, a long-sleeved turtleneck

Cut a slit in the side of the hem of a pillowcase. Insert elastic through this slit and thread it through the entire hem. Adjust the elastic to fit the waist of the child and secure it with a safety pin. This will be the skirt. Cut off the closed end of the pillowcase so that it comes close to the floor. (Illus. 6) The other pillowcase will be the tunic which goes over the turtleneck. Cut a hole out of the closed end of the pillowcase for the head. Cut holes on the sides for arms. Cut off the open end of the pillowcase as needed to adjust for height. (Illus. 7) Tie a long, thin piece of fabric around the child's waist and over both shoulders. Cross it in front and tie it back around the waist. (Illus. 8)

Illus. 8

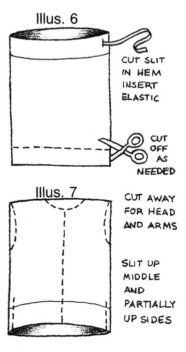

Illus. 6

CUT SLIT IN HEM INSERT ELASTIC

CUT OFF AS NEEDED

Illus. 7

CUT AWAY FOR HEAD AND ARMS

SLIT UP MIDDLE AND PARTIALLY UP SIDES

 Tikki Tikki Tembo

The 2 brothers, Ping Ping, Ling Ling, and members of the chorus: pillowcase or man's shirt, fabric to tie at waist, pajama bottoms or slacks

Create a tunic by cutting one hole out of the closed end of a pillowcase for the head and a hole on each side of the pillowcase for arms. If pillowcases are not available, each child can wear a man's shirt that can be cut down to fit as a tunic. (Illus. 7) Children can decorate these if desired. Pajama bottoms or slacks are worn under the tunics. Tie the tunics at the waist.

Old Man: pillowcase or man's shirt, fabric to tie at waist, pajama bottoms or slacks, brown yarn, tag board, elastic thread

The old man's costume will be the same as that of the two brothers but will have the following additions: Cut a piece of tag board to fit across the chin of the child. The shape will be that of a quarter moon. Color this piece with brown marker. Use a hole punch to put holes all over the piece. Cut pieces of rug yarn to fit through the holes and hang down. Tie a knot in one end of each piece to hold it. Shape the beard so that it is longer in the middle. Attach a piece of elastic thread to the sides of the beard and tie them in loops to fit over the child's ears. (Illus. 9)

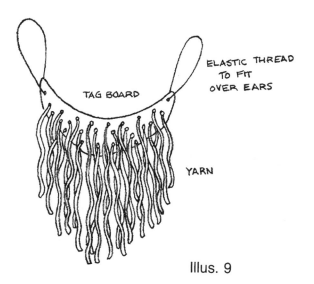

Illus. 9

The following roles are optional:

Well Holders: Brown shirt and pants, 4 pieces of cardboard, yarn, brown paper.

Two children wear brown outfits. Make placards for them to wear by balling up brown paper and gluing it onto the cardboard. Place one piece of cardboard in front of each child and one piece in back. Attach the two boards with yarn over the child's shoulders. Make a crown of "stones" by wrapping a strip of brown paper around each child's head and attaching balled-up pieces of paper to the headband. (Illus. 10)

Illus. 10

Flowers: Green shirt and pants, paper plates, construction paper, yarn.

Dress children in green shirts and pants. Cut the center out of paper plates and attach yarn to fit around the head of each child. Cut out petal shapes from construction paper and glue or staple around edge of paper plates. (Illus. 11)

Illus. 11

9   Tikki Tikki Tembo

SET DESIGN

The children can play a part in planning the stage design as they explore this drama set to music. Discuss what objects should appear on stage and in the background. Talk about how big the objects on stage will be, what the well will look like, and how it will be built. Decide how large the set needs to be for the audience to see clearly.

Use masking tape to mark places on the stage for the chorus, the well, the tree, Ling Ling, Ping Ping, and Mother.

The chorus stands to each side of the stage area. The Chinese orchestra, whose members are also part of the chorus, can sit on both sides in front of the chorus. Provide chairs for the orchestra so that the members can place their instruments under their chairs when the instruments are not in use.

The narrator stands in front, stage left, facing the audience.

The backdrop can be two bulletin boards. Cover the board that is stage right with a mural of a mountain with a tree on it. The other bulletin board can have a mural of a mountain with a house on it and a stream flowing at the foot of the mountain.

The stream flowing stage left can be crepe paper streamers in shades of blue laid on the floor. The mother is working in front of the stream.

The well is situated in the center, a little toward stage right. It can be drawn on heavy corrugated cardboard, painted, and cut out with a craft knife. If desired, two children can hold up the well.

Ling Ling and Ping Ping are located toward the center, stage right. The flowers can be potted plants, flowers the children have made, or even children with flower hats. The kite can be suspended from the ceiling ahead of time. Attach a string to it that the child who plays Ping Ping can hold.

The tree can be cut out of heavy corrugated cardboard and painted. It can be attached to a high-backed chair so it is free standing. The old man sits in front of it.

The brothers start at stage right with their mother and work their way across the stage as needed for the story.

 Tikki Tikki Tembo

STEP-BY-STEP (YOU CAN DO IT!)

1. Read the story of *Tikki Tikki Tembo*.
2. Dramatize the story.
3. Teach children the difference between a play and a musical.
4. Introduce the narration and songs from the musical.
5. Assign parts by picking out children who want to act and seem comfortable in the roles.
6. Choose a narrator from the class if you have a strong reader, otherwise choose another adult for the role.
7. Decide whether to use the CD or an accompanist.
8. Practice parts and songs separately and together.
9. Design and make set and costumes.
10. Plan and have a dress rehearsal.
11. Production.

Total time allowed will depend on how much of the accompanying curriculum you will include in your preparation. Minimum time allowed for the basic musical is about two weeks. If you plan to use the curriculum ideas and prepare the performance allow about a month. Have fun!

11   Tikki Tikki Tembo

NARRATION

(Opening Song)

Many years ago in China, there was a little boy who had a very long name. His name was Tikki Tikki Tembo-No So Rembo-Icka Na Noo Na-Konna Ron Tombo. *(Name Chant)*

The boy's younger brother had a short little name—Wing. Wing wished he had a long and honorable name like his brother, Tikki Tikki Tembo-No So Rembo-Icka Na Noo Na-Konna Ron Tombo. *(Name Chant)*

The two brothers liked to play outside while their mother washed clothes in the river. *(Washing Song)*

One day the two boys were playing too close to a well and Wing fell in. His brother ran to Mother who was by the river. *(Help Song)*

"Speak louder!" said Mother. "The river is noisy!" *(River Song)*

So Tikki Tikki Tembo-No So Rembo-Icka Na Noo Na-Konna Ron Tombo used his very loud voice. *(Help Song)*

"Then hurry!" shouted Mother. "Find the old man with the long rope. Ask him to get your brother out of the well."

So off the boy ran. Soon he came to Ling Ling who was picking flowers. "Ling Ling, help!" *(Have You Seen the Old Man?)*

Ling Ling shook her head and said, "I don't know where he is."

 Tikki Tikki Tembo

So off ran Tikki Tikki Tembo-No So Rembo-Icka Na Noo Na-Konna Ron Tombo. Soon he came to Ping Ping who was flying a kite.

"Ping Ping, help!" *(Have You Seen the Old Man?)*

Ping Ping pointed. "He's over there sleeping under the old tree."

Tikki Tikki Tembo-No So Rembo-Icka Na Noo Na-Konna Ron Tombo ran off. *(Name Chant)*

He ran to the old tree. There he found the old man sleeping. The boy tried to wake him. *(Wake Up Song)*

The old man slept on, so the boy used his very loud voice. *(Wake Up Song)*

The old man woke up. And when he heard about Wing, he grabbed his long rope and hobbled to the well.

The man threw the rope over the side of the well. Down it went into the well, and up climbed poor wet Wing. Wing coughed a little cough and soon felt fine.

But a few days later, the two boys played by the well again. This time the brother with the long and honorable name fell into the well! Wing ran to his mother at the river. *(Help Song)*

"Speak louder!" said Mother. "The river is noisy!" *(River Song)*

   Tikki Tikki Tembo

So Wing used his very loud voice. *(Help Song)*

"Who fell into the well?" she asked.

Poor Wing tried to say the long name as fast as he could. "Tikki Tikki Noo Na . . . I mean Tikki Stikki popcorn . . . I mean . . ."

His mother shouted, "Do you mean that the person in the well is Tikki Tikki Tembo-No So Rembo-Icka Na Noo Na-Konna Ron Tombo?" *(Name Chant)*

"Yes," said Wing.

"Then hurry!" shouted Mother. "Find the old man with the long rope. Ask him to get your brother out of the well."

Wing ran off.

Soon he came to Ling Ling who was picking flowers. "Ling Ling, help!" *(Have You Seen the Old Man?)*

Ling Ling shook her head and said, "I don't know where he is."

So off ran Wing. Soon he came to Ping Ping who was flying a kite.

"Ping Ping, help!" *(Have You Seen the Old Man?)*

Ping Ping pointed. "He's over there sleeping under the old tree."

Wing ran to the old tree. There he found the old man sleeping. The boy tried to wake him. *(Wake Up Song)*

The old man slept on, so Wing used his very loud voice. *(Wake Up Song)*

The old man began to snore. *(Snoring Song)*

Tikki Tikki Tembo

So Wing shook him and shook him until he finally woke up. The boy shouted, "My brother is in the well. Please help Tikki Tikki Tembo-No So Rembo-Icka Na Noo Na-Konna Ron Tombo." *(Name Chant)*

"Who?" asked the old man, yawning.

"Wing yelled in his loudest voice, "Tikki Tikki Tembo-No So Rembo-Icka Na Noo Na-Konna Ron Tombo." *(Name Chant)*

The old man grabbed his long rope and hobbled to the well. He threw the rope into the well, but nobody climbed up. The old man went down into the well and slowly carried the boy up the rope. The boy was very full of water, so the old man pushed and pushed the water out of him.

Poor Tikki Tikki Tembo-No So Rembo-Icka Na Noo Na-Konna Ron Tombo was sick for many days. He had been in the well for a long time. His long and honorable name had been hard to say, so Wing had not been able to get him help quickly. When Tikki Tikki Tembo-No So Rembo-Icka Na Noo Na-Konna Ron Tombo was better, his mother decided to give him a short little name. She called him Tick. And Wing was happy that his name was just Wing.

And Chinese mothers from that day on have given short and honorable names to all their children.

So...all's well that ends well. *(All's Well That Ends Well)*

Tikki Tikki Tembo

MUSICAL SCORE

OPENING SONG

Sung by Chorus

16   Tikki Tikki Tembo

Tikki Tikki Tembo

NAME CHANT

Slowly

Chanted by Chorus

Cymbal Crash (pot lids)

Tik-ki Tik-ki Tem-bo—No So Rem-bo—Ic-ka Na Noo Na—Kon-na Ron Tom-bo.

WASHING SONG

Blues-like

Sung by A⁷ Mother and Chorus

Ev-'ry day I wash the clothes. My

sons get dir-ty from heads to toes. There's mud on these pants, and

Tikki Tikki Tembo

19   Tikki Tikki Tembo

HELP SONG

20   Tikki Tikki Tembo

RIVER SONG

Sung by
Mother and Chorus

The riv-er is swish-ing and swash-ing and swirl-ing. The riv-er is twist-ing and tumb-ling and twirl-ing out to the sea, out to the sea.

21   Tikki Tikki Tembo

HAVE YOU SEEN THE OLD MAN?

WAKE UP SONG

Moderate speed

Sung by Tikki Wing and Chorus

Wake up! Wake up! Please o-pen your eyes. The sun's in the sky. It's time to rise. Wake rise.

         Tikki Tikki Tembo

SNORING SONG

Tikki Tikki Tembo

Tikki Tikki Tembo

ALL'S WELL THAT ENDS WELL

Sung by Entire Cast

All's well that ends well. What more can we say? Bad things will change and will go a-way. And we will have a hap-pi-er day. So all's well that ends well, what more can we say? You spill your milk out of your cup. Some-one helps you to clean it up. The

Tikki Tikki Tembo

27   Tikki Tikki Tembo

LYRICS TO SONGS

OPENING SONG
(Sung by chorus)

Here is a tale of a boy and his name,
Boy and his name, boy and his name.
Here is a tale of a boy and his name,
A short little boy with a long name.

Chorus:
A name can be short.
A name can be long.
A name is a name,
so what can go wrong?
What can go wrong?
Isn't it the same
If a name is a short
Or a long name?

This happened in China many years ago,
Many years ago, many years ago.
This happened in China many years ago
To a short little boy
With a long name.

Chorus

(at end add:)
Lo----------ng name. Long name!

NAME CHANT
(Chanted by chorus)

(This chant is repeated several times throughout the musical. A crash of cymbals—or pot lids—by the narrator or a child who listens well to cues announces the "Name Chant.")

(Crash of cymbals)
Tikki Tikki Tembo-
No So Rembo-
Icka Na Noo Na-
Konna Ron Tombo

WASHING SONG
(Sung by Mother and chorus)

Ev'ry day I wash the clothes.
My sons get dirty
From heads to toes.
There's mud on these pants
And food on this shirt.
This mother is tired of
washing out dirt.

Chorus:
I wash and scrub and squeeze,
Always on my knees.
How my hands do hurt, hurt, hurt,
Rubbing out this dirty dirt.
I wash and scrub and squeeze,
Always on my knees.

HELP SONG
(Sung by Tikki/Wing and chorus)

Help! Help!
Brother's in the well.
He got too close
and in he fell.
Help! Help!
Brother's in the well.
What shall we do
and whom shall we tell?

RIVER SONG
(Sung by Mother and chorus)

The river is swishing
And swashing and swirling.
The river is twisting
and tumbling and twirling
Out to the sea,
Out to the sea.

HAVE YOU SEEN THE OLD MAN?
(Sung by Tikki/Wing and chorus)

Have you seen the old man,
The old man and the rope?
Have you seen the old man?
I hope. I hope. I hope.

(Repeat)

Tikki Tikki Tembo

WAKE UP SONG
(Sung by Tikki/Wing and chorus)

Wake up! Wake up!
Please open your eyes.
The sun's in the sky
It's time to rise.

(Repeat)

SNORING SONG
(Sung by Old Man and chorus)

Sleepy time can be such a bore
Unless you open your mouth and snore.
Snore this. (snore, snore)
Snore that. (snore, snore)
Snore a whistle. (snore, whistle)
Snore a cat. (snore, meow)
Snore a chicken. (snore, bauk bauk)
Snore a cheer. (snore, yay)
Snoring is great
If there's no one to hear.

ALL'S WELL THAT ENDS WELL
(Sung by entire cast)

Chorus:
All's well that ends well.
What more can we say?
Bad things will change
and will go away.
And we will have a happier day.
So all's well that ends well.
What more can we say?

You spill your milk out of your cup.
Someone helps you to clean it up.
The heel comes off of your favorite shoe.
You fix it up with a little glue.
You fall in a well and feel like a dope.
Someone throws you a long, long rope.

Chorus

(at end, add:)
Well, I know...(spoken)
Thank you for coming to see our play!

30   Tikki Tikki Tembo

ADDITIONAL ACTIVITIES AND DISCUSSION TOPICS

Discuss relationships within the family.
> The position of the children from oldest to youngest
> Dividing the attention of parents among the children
> Who feels special? Who feels left out? Why?

Discuss the importance of a name.
> Why is it important to have a name?
> What would it be like without names?
> How do we shorten names?
> How do we choose names for people?

Bake Fortune Tea Cakes by making muffins and baking fortunes in them.

Discuss Bamboo.
> Importance to Chinese
> Pandas
> Uses

Discuss kinds of fabrics and how they are made.
> Silk from the silkworm
> Cotton from the cotton boll

Plan an imaginary trip to visit China.
> Show China on a globe and discuss how to get there.
> Make a suitcase and travel supplies out of construction paper. Pack the suitcase.
> Make tickets and write basic travel information on them (name, date, destination, etc.).
> Plan a Bon Voyage party. Serve clear soda and fish crackers if you plan to travel by boat.
> Pretend to board a ship or plane. Create a tape of all the information that a captain or pilot would give to passengers.
> Pretend to arrive in Beijing, China's capital city, during the New Year Festival. Discuss what you would see.

Discuss the lunar calendar.
> Compare it to our calendar.
> Each year is named for a sign of the zodiac.
> Talk about the symbol for this year.

     Tikki Tikki Tembo

BIBLIOGRAPHY

Adshead, Robin. *China*

A Living Here Book. *We Live in China*

Ayer, Jacqueline. *Little Silk*

Ayer, Jacqueline. *Nu Dang and His Kite*

Behrens, Jane. *Gung Hay Fat Choy*

Bishop, Claire. *Five Chinese Brothers*

Borja, Robert. *Making Chinese Papercuts*

Brown, Shirley. *Around the World Stories to Tell to Children*

Brown, Tricia. *Chinese New Year*

Carpenter, Frances. *Tales of a Chinese Grandmother*

Carter, Michael. *Crafts of China*

Filstrip, Chris and Jamie. *China from Emperors to Communes*

Fisher, Leonard. *The Great Wall of China*

Flack, Marjorie & Wiese, Kurt. *The Story About Ping*

Fyson, Nance Lui. *A Family in China*

Hardendorff, Jeanne B. *The Frog's Saddle Horse and Other Tales*

How-Tien, Cheng. *The Chinese New Year*

Hughes-Stanton, Penelope. *An Ancient Chinese Town*

Kimishino. *Lum Fu and the Golden Mountain*

Kuo, Louise and Yuan Hsi. *Chinese Folk Tales*

Lee, Jeanne. *Legend of the Milky Way*

Lyrichord Discs, Inc. *Chinese Opera and Folk Themes*

Martin, Patricia. *The Rice Bowl Pet*

Mosel, Arlene. *Tikki Tikki Tembo*

National Association of Junior Chatauquas. *Through Storyland with Children*

Polite, Leo. *Mr. Fong's Toy Shop*

Stone, Jon. *Big Bird in China*

Time-Life Books. *Chinese Cooking*

Wolkstein, Dianne. *8,000 Stones*

Yashima. *Crow Boy*

Yashima. *Momo's Kitten*

Yungnei, Tang. *China, Here We Come!*